CHURCH PLATE
FROM THE COLLECTIONS
OF THE NATIONAL MUSEUM OF HISTORY

CHURCH PLATE

FROM
THE COLLECTIONS
OF
THE NATIONAL MUSEUM
OF HISTORY

introduced by
Teofana Matakieva-Lilkova

BORINA

Published in 1995 by Borina Publishing House
P.O.Box 105; 1408 Sofia; Bulgaria

ISBN 954 500 061 9

The Orthodox church locks the space of mystery and mysticism. It is a majestic artistic ensemble which is called to give esthetic enjoyment and elevate the souls of believers to heaven.

The deliberate incorporation of objets d'art in religious practices seeks to bring spiritual grandeur to believers. The church plate are utterly different from the cult relics that had been in prior use. The church plate are designed to hold part of the divine body and blood of Jesus, and as such are the immediate bearer of divine energy. The main vocation of art is not to beautify the church or re-translate historical and theological information but help divine knowledge while being involved in the divine service itself and possessing divine energy as it combines magic identity and prototype and exists for and by the viewer.

The artistic symbol that is embodied in a peculiar plastic and color and rhythm image creates the illusion of transcendentalism.

Bulgaria that lies on the crossroads between the East and West can claim links with the earliest Christian civilization. As the new religion struck roots in the Balkans, Christian communities were formed in the first few centuries, hence the church council that took place in Serdica in 343.

When the Proto-Bulgarians founded the Bulgarian state together with the Slavs in the 7th century, they encountered plenty of evidence of Christian art on these lands. Moreover, the proximity of Byzantium and its leading role in the history of the old world determined the orientation of the first Bulgarian rulers to the Christian East.

King Boris I's exceptional political vision put Bulgaria in the van of Christendom. In 865 Bulgaria was the first among the Slavs to adopt Christianity as an official religion from Byzantium. This was related to another culturally historic event, the introduction of the Slavonic script that the Thessalonian brothers Cyril and Methodius invented and their disciples, the so-called Holy Seven, disseminated. When in the 9th century Bulgaria joined Christendom it was closely linked with Christian cultural history while the crossroads geographic location between the East and West integrated into Bulgarian art the connections with and dissimilarity from the Orthodox art in the other Christian lands.

The first masters who built and decorated Christian churches after the conversion to the new religion came from Byzantium. Bulgarian Christian art heritage is related to Byzantine classical and esthetic tenets. Most of the churches in the period in question were lavishly gorgeous. Remember the interior decoration comprising painted ceramic tiles, geometric floral ornamentation and animal figures or elements. Add to this profuse picture the stone carving outside comprising Antiquity elements, Christian symbolism and the teratological style of the settlers.

The biggest Bulgarian monastery in the proximity of St John of Rila's hermitage in the Rila Mountain was founded in the time of the First Bulgarian Kingdom. The earliest "popular" life of the saint from the 12th century tells that the Bulgarian king Peter went to pay homage to the hermit and sent precious gifts one of which was a gold chalice.

Church art flowered again in the Second Bulgarian Kingdom that was re-established in late 12th century after the victorious uprising of the brothers Assen and Peter. The Bulgarian Patriarchate was re-established correspondingly. Many churches and monasteries were built in the new royal city, Turnovgrad, and around it. Erudite men of letters who were followers or pupils of patriarch Euthymius carried out a literary reform. Their work had an impact on the culture of all Orthodox Slav people of Serbia, Wallachia, Moldavia and Russia. An eminent proof of the heyday of that culture is provided by the works of the Turnovo painting school.

A repousse of a gospel with exquisite composition, high relief, classical proportions and figures is a remarkable example of 14th century Balkan goldsmithery which is to be traced to the Constantinople workshops. The nielo technique on several tiles that were additionally inserted in the 17th century likewise suggests kinship with the Byzantine tradition. St Clement and St Pantaleimon in full size were added at a later date. The bodies have shortened proportions, heavy figures that were characteristic of the later period and big heads with wide open expressive eyes. The style is quite different from the manner of master Nikola who made most of the repousse in the 14th century.

The efflorescence of 14th century Christian culture in the Balkans was related to two art tendencies. The official tendency stood for excellent professionalism and was supported by the state aristocracy and the high-ranking ecclesiastics. The provincial tendency was primitive but expressive and emotional.

Extermination, forcible displacement, assimilatory policy, conversions to Islam, destruction of the big Christian churches and monasteries were the main methods of the invaders' expansion. The statehood of the Balkan states was abolished.

The fall of the capital city, Turnovo, in 1393 and the conquest of all Bulgaria in 1396 put an end to the official line of cultural development. The Orthodox church, the only institution that survived, played a historic role in saving the Balkan nations that lived in bondage after the fall of Constantinople in 1453.

The church organized, maintained and inspired cultural life in the new situation of ordeal. In default of official state support art had ups and downs. Churches and monasteries collected donations from people, commissioned still known artists and encouraged art as much as they could.

Monasteries were feudal estates and although many of them were stripped of their privileges, remained such in the times of bondage. The bigger ones, like the Rila Monastery, were honored traditionally with gifts by the Turkish sultans.

The monasteries were the main strongholds of Bulgarian culture and that was their most essential role in the years of Ottoman domination. They kept holy relics, medieval treasures, manuscripts, icons and lovely church plate reminiscent of the glorious past, not remote at that, of the Bulgarians and their state. Some monasteries were art centers where the humble means of the population maintained tradition. Also the monasteries maintained educational and cultural relations with other Balkan monasteries and churches, with the monastic republic of Mount Athos which was the leading art center for the orthodox world.

Eminent ecclesiastics and notables from other Christian Balkan lands sent gifts to the Bulgarian monasteries. Some of the exquisite objects and church plate that the Bachkovo Monastery possesses were made by Italian, to be more precise, by Venetian goldsmiths. The best goldsmiths were commissioned to make the repousse for the Kroupnitsa and Suchava gospels that the Rila Monastery got as presents.

Sofia was a literary center in the 16th century. It produced original works about the newly canonized Sofia martyrs who died for their faith. Priest Peyo wrote a service and a life of Georgi, a goldsmith of Sofia, who came to be known later as Georgi Novi Sofiiski. He was burnt alive in 1515 at the Church of St Sophia for he refused to renounce his religion.

The Sofia goldsmithery school of that time had a singular style and kinship to the primitive trend in art.

Relations between the Bulgarian and Athonite monasteries, particularly with the Zographou Monastery and Hilendar Monastery, intensified in the 16th and 17th century. Many monks went from place to place in the Bulgarian lands, distributed books, opened branches of monasteries and schools, brought together pilgrims, collected donations, sought cooperation with other free Christian countries. The monasteries were the cradle of historical memory, of the glorious medieval past and statehood, and fostered religion, literature, culture and nationhood in the darkest times for Bulgarians.

The 17th century was the beginning of a flowering period for Bulgarian towns which became the major manufacturers in the declining Ottoman Empire. Trade relations with cities in central and western Europe continually intensified and expanded. The Bulgarian people became richer, and arts developed correspondingly. Chiprovtsi, a Catholic center, was the leader in goldsmithery in the Bulgarian lands and in the Balkans. Influences of western Catholic and Gothic art can be traced in the Chiprovtsi goldsmiths' works. A typical feature is the miniature-like inscribed figures of saints in a profuse filigree geometric lacework. Lamps and other church plate have been found in Bulgarian churches and monasteries and also in the Dechani sacristy and in the sacristy of the monastery in Banya in Patmos. The famous 16th century Dechani pyx is the best work that this school has produced. The pyx is made of massive gold-plated silver, has the shape of a dome church and dozens of scenes from the Bible, some of which measure 1/1 cm are interwoven into the exquisite lacework of over 300 elements. The plastic figures of dragons, nude caryatids other fabulous creatures that the severe canon and Eastern Orthodox scholasticism would not allow are remarkable.

The graceful miniature-like figures, the profusion of scenes, their severe composition and plastic idiom suggest a virtuoso. The magnificent decoration is reinforced by the colorful stones that are set at random and create solemnity and effulgence.

Vratsa was a famous goldsmithery center. The crosses, pyxes and chalices that have come down to us show that form tended to be graphic and austere.

The other contemporary goldsmith workshops produce the same impression. More often than not the objects are explicitly graphic and flatly ornamented, with manifest severe grace, exquisite form and architectonics. These are the crosses of hieromonk Averki from 1615, master Kaspar from 1648 and master Konstantin from 1774.

In the second half of the 18th century the Ottoman Empire was rent by internal contradictions, financial problems and degenerate military system and so declined further. The Empire's cultural development was far behind that of Europe. The progressive spirit that the prospering trade and industries generated in Europe clashed with the rigid Ottoman feudal ways that disagreed with the new time. The Bulgarian population that had always been part of the European civilization which is a successor of the century-long traditions in the Balkans and the Mediterranean world with their millennial Christian tradition quickly adjusted to the new technical discoveries and were keenly interested in the achievements of western culture. The Bulgarians were enterprising in all areas of economic and cultural life. They were merchants and among the best manufacturers in the Balkans. They manufactured clocks for clock towers, big candlesticks of wrought iron, bells, famous carpets and traded with Egypt, Syria, Romania, Greece, Russia, Southern France, Austria and Italy. Bulgarian merchant centers were established in Bucharest, Istanbul, Marseilles, Moscow, Odessa, Budapest and Vienna. In their native places they built churches, schools and big baroque-style houses. Literature, art, music and education flourished.

The Bulgarian monk Paissi wrote The Slav-Bulgarian History in the Hilendar Monastery in 1762 to re-awake the national identity and dignity of his countrymen.

A new art trend evolved in Mount Athos in the 18th century. It brought in one the old eastern traditions, the elements of the Italo-Cretan school and western baroque and exerted influence on orthodox art in the Balkans.

A new distinguished church was built in the Rila Monastery after a devastating fire in 1833. It was the focal point of the best achievements of art of the day. The monastery was built with the effort and money of Bulgarians from all parts of the country. The precious possessions comprise hundreds of exquisite works of the goldsmith art: crosses, lamps, chalices and reliquaries that had been presented by guilds or individually, by pilgrims to this Bulgarian sanctuary from all corners of the Balkans and Mount Athos.

The influences of Western Europe can be conspicuously traced in Bulgarian church art which abounds in ornamentation, volume and fretwork baroque elements that are occasionally taken to the extreme. Flowers, roses, clusters of grapes, vines, all the fruit of the bountiful Bulgarian land are interwoven.

The nature of the Orthodox Church and its millennial history predetermined the mission of church art, its democratic disposition and consistent abidance by tradition. Relics of venerated saints translated from near and far Balkan lands, writings in Bulgarian, miracle-working icons and precious plate are kept there. The church was a treasury, patron and supporter of the arts. That culture was related to the apostolic lifework of the Thessalonian brothers Cyril and Methodius, their disciples Clement and Nahum, the music of John Koukouzeles and the works of Pimen Zograf.

This art with millennial tradition has always served the lofty idea of saving the worthy Bulgarian potential, intellect, esthetics and mentality. It is a cache keeping fabulous wealth that waits to be unlocked. That wealth comprises the clumsy primitive gifts of peasants and the magnificent royal gifts. All this is evidence of the creative manifold Bulgarian genius and talent. In time of pogrom, fire and destruction many of these precious possessions were carefully and considerately taken to other locations. Secretly and with fervor they were handed down from generation to generation before they came down to us for our forefathers knew and appreciated their magic power which is their never-fading value and ability to guard and support us. They are the link between the past and the future, the dignity of the centuries that were and the hope of the centuries that will be. Therefore it is our duty to guard and hand them down to the generation to come.

Teofana Matakieva-Lilkova, Senior Research Associate

1. Rhipide Christ the Ruler of the
Universe, 1594, donor's inscription, silver, gilding, enamel, diam.
23 cm, invt. No 29216

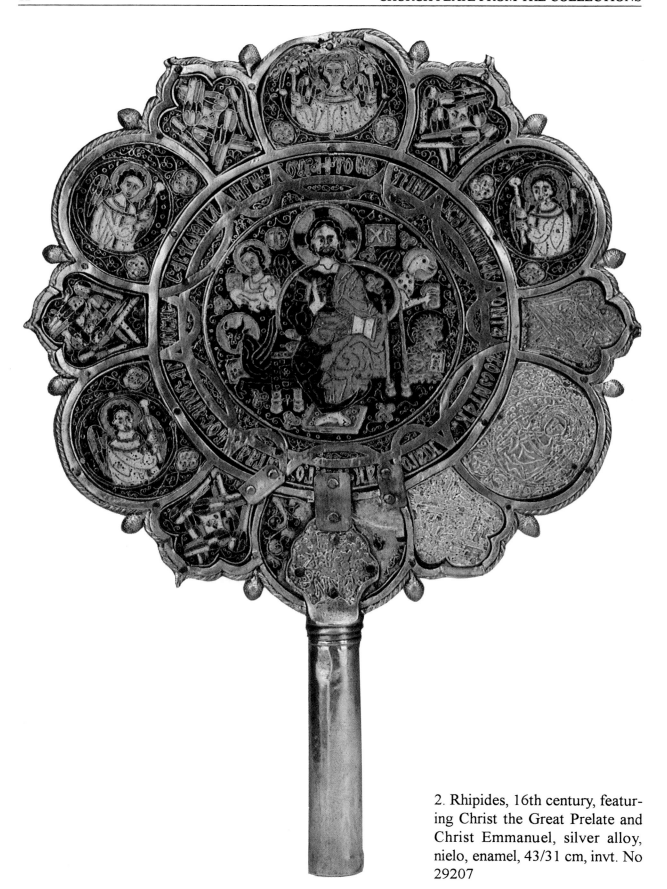

2. Rhipides, 16th century, featuring Christ the Great Prelate and Christ Emmanuel, silver alloy, nielo, enamel, 43/31 cm, invt. No 29207

3. Rhipides, 16th century, featuring Christ the Great Prelate and Christ Emmanuel, silver alloy, nielo, enamel, 43/31 cm, invt. No 29207

4. Rhipide Christ Emmanuel, 1594, donor's inscription, silver, gilding, enamel, diam. 23 cm, invt. No 29216

5. Cross, 1615, donor's inscription, master hieromonk Averki, miniature wood carving, silver with gilding, inlaid stones, 8.5/21/3 cm, invt. No 29153

6. Cross, 1618, donor's inscription, wood carving, repousse of silver alloy with gilding, 35/12.5 cm, invt. No 29173

7. Pyx, 1626, Dechani Monastery, silver, gilding, enamel, color stones, Chiprovtsi goldsmithery school, size 30/25 cm, invt. No 29211

8. Reliquary, 1630, featuring The Ascension, silver alloy with gilding, 26.5/19/6.5 cm, invt. No 29174

9. Cross, 1648, donor's inscription, master Kaspar, commissioned by the town of Seres, miniature wood carving, repousse of gold-plated filigree, coral, 13/29/2.5 cm, invt. No 29175

10. Cross, 17th century, miniature
wood carving, repousse with
gold-plated filigree, color stone,
cellular enamel, in a wooden box,
29.5/16.5 cm, invt. No 29186

11. Repousse of an icon of St George with scenes from his life, 17th century, silver alloy with gilding, diam. 25 cm, invt. No 29047

12. Reliquary of St Dionysius the Patriarch of Constantinople with scenes from the Bible and saints, 1744, donor's inscription, silver, gilding, 31/23/27 cm, invt. No 29115

13. Repousse of a skull, death mask, 1744, silver, gilding, nielo, invt. No 29115

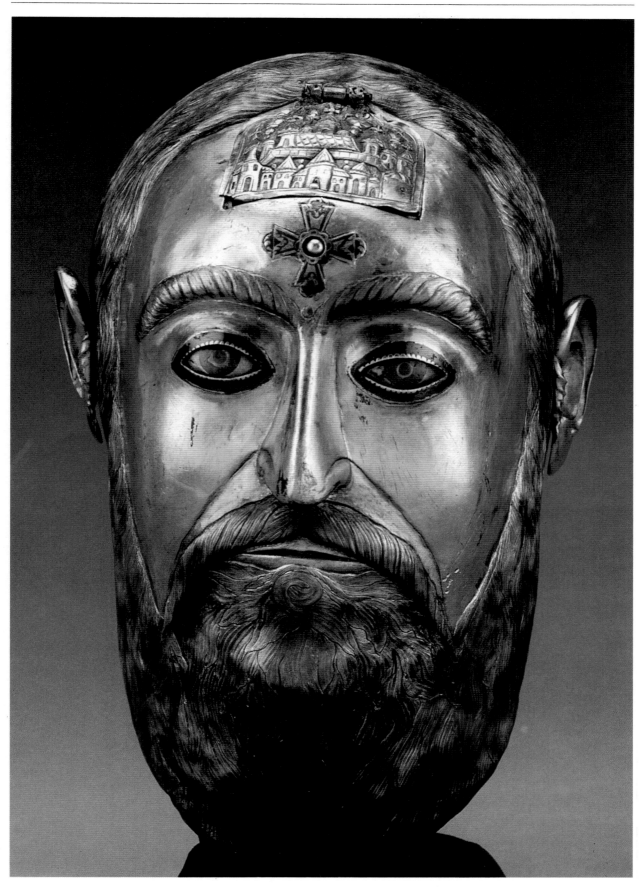

14. Chalice, 1731, donor's inscription, silver, gilding, floral motifs and birds, ht. 26 cm, invt. No 29067

15. Censer, 1763, donor's inscription, silver, ht. 23.5 cm, diam. 11.5 cm, invt. No 29136

16. Reliquary featuring Christ the Ruler of the Universe and SS Constantine and Hellen, 1765, silver alloy with gilding, relief decoration, 30.5/14/3.5 cm, invt. No 29168

17. Repousse of the icon The Virgin Showing the Way, 1765, silver alloy, 108/60 cm, invt. No 29041

18. Reliquary whose lid features the Holy Trinity, 1773, silver alloy, plastic decoration, 34/29/7 cm, invt. No 29210

19. Cross, 1774, donor's inscription, master Konstantin Stoyanov, miniature carving, repousse, gold-plated filigree, color stones, 28.5/12.5 cm, invt. No 29178

20. Lamp, 1776, silver, ht. 68 cm, invt. No 29213

21. Reliquary, St Dionysius, St John Chrysostom, St Pantaleimon, St Andrew the First Called, 1783, donor's inscription, silver, gilding, copper base, 25.5/18/10 cm, invt. No 29194

22. Cross, 1786, silver, gilding, color stones and corals, 57/23 cm, invt. No 29185

23. Service vessel featuring The
Baptism of Christ and The Virgin
with Apostles, 1787, donor's inscription, master Nikolaya, silver,
gilding, ht. 32 cm, diam. 27.5 cm,
invt. No 29124, 29126

24. Lamp, 1789, donor's inscription. silver, ht. 40 cm, diam. 24 cm, invt. No 29212

25. Repousse to an icon of the Virgin, 1789, silver alloy, color stones, 28/20 cm, invt. No 29082

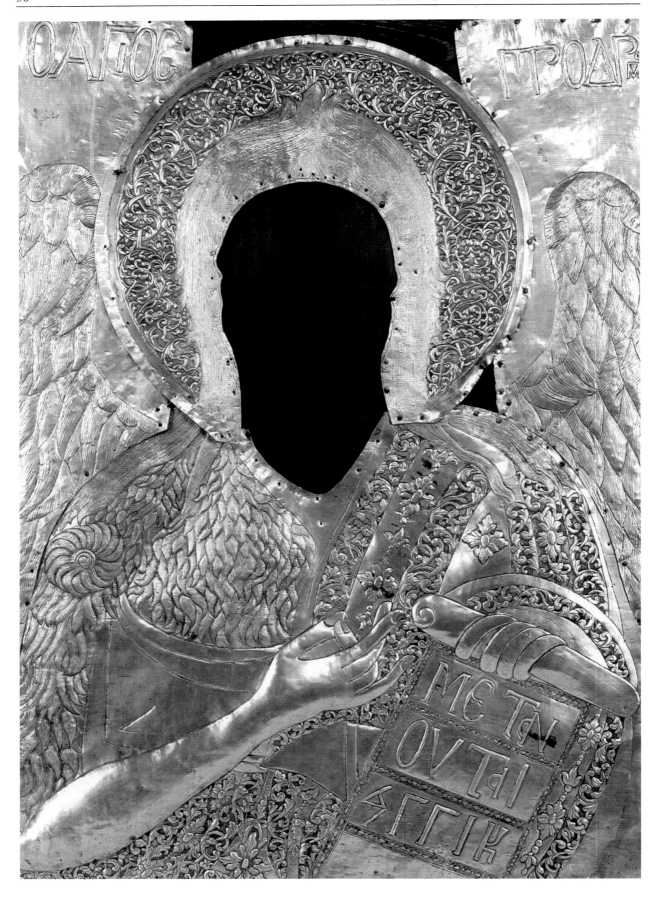

26. Repousse of the icon of John the Precursor, 18th century, silver alloy, 84/64 cm, invt. No 29042

27. Cross, 18th century, wood carving, repousse from silver alloy, corals, 16/9 cm, invt. No 29161

28. Reliquary of St Haralampi,
18th century, donor's inscription,
silver, gilding, 9/6/2 cm, invt. No
29167

29. Repousse to an icon of the
Virgin, 18th century, silver alloy
with gilding, color stones, 22.5/
17 cm, invt. No 29184

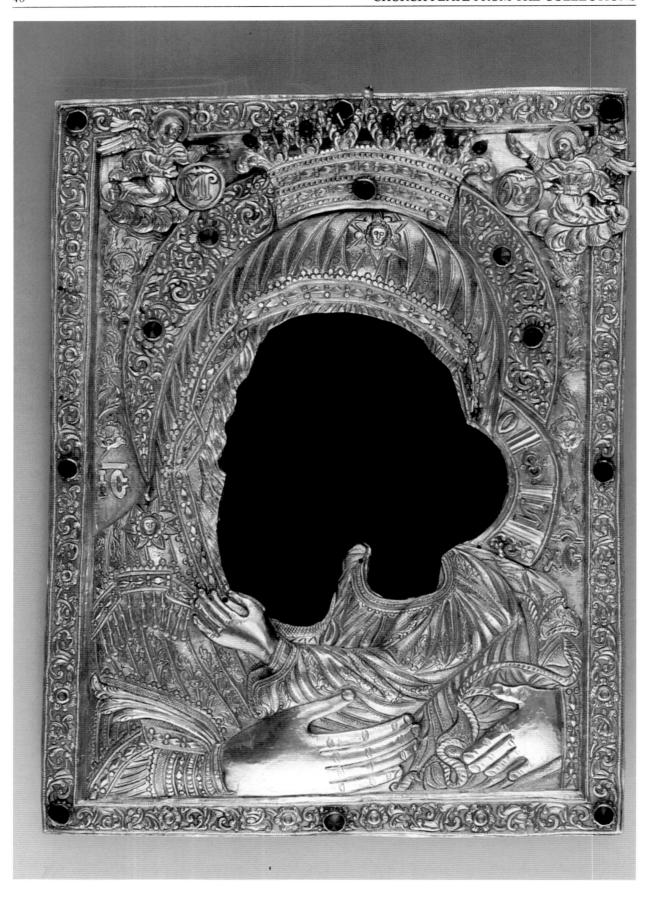

30. Repousse to an icon of Our Lady of Tenderness, 18th century, silver alloy with gilding, color stones, 27.5/20.5 cm, invt. No 29183

31. Cross, 18th century donor's inscription, silver, gilding, stones, 67/30 cm, invt. No 29189

32. Reliquary, 18th century, silver, gilding, 11.5/4.5/3.5 cm, invt. No 29166

33. Cross, 18th century, silver, gilding, Christ's feasts, 22/13.5 cm, invt. No 29131

34. Repousse featuring St John the Precursor with scenes from his life, 18th century, silver, gilding. 150/130 cm, invt. No 29054, 29053

35. Reliquary, 18th century, silver, gilding, donor's inscription, 16/ 6.5/2.5 cm, invt. No 29163

36. Reliquary of St Dionysius, 18th century, donor's inscription, silver, gilding, 13.5/5.5/3.5 cm, invt. No 29156

37. Bishop's crosier, 18th century, black lacquered wood, silver, gilding, length 165 cm, invt. No 29197

38. Reliquary of St Trifon, 18th century, donor's inscription, silver, gilding, 18.5/5.5/4 cm, invt. No 29155

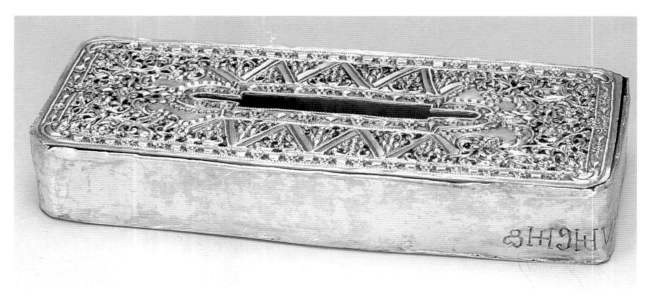

39. Bishop's belt featuring The Virgin with Prophets, second half of the 18th century, 13 plates, silver, gilding, length 74 cm, invt. No 29075

40. Lamp, second half of the 18th century, silver alloy, 19/10.5 cm, invt. No 29146

41. Lamp, second half of the 18th century, silver, ht. 22 cm, diam. 10.5 cm, invt. No 29140

42. Censer, 18th-19th century, silver, copper, ht. 25 cm, diam. 12 cm, invt. No 29130

43. Cross, 18th-19th century, gilded filigree, granulation, stones, 8/16 cm, invt. No 29962

44. Reliquary - offertory box, with an icon the Virgin Showing the Way, 18th-19th century, wood, tempera, repousse, silver, gilding, 13/10.5/2.5 cm, invt. No 29191

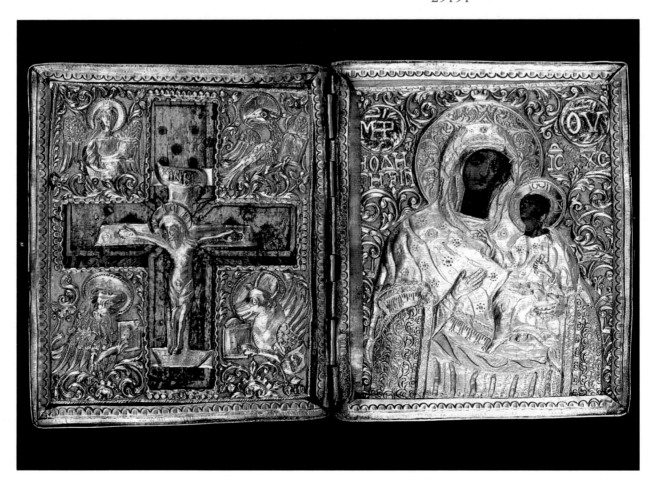

45. Bishop's crosier, 19th century, brass, gilding, stones, length 170 cm, invt. No 29105

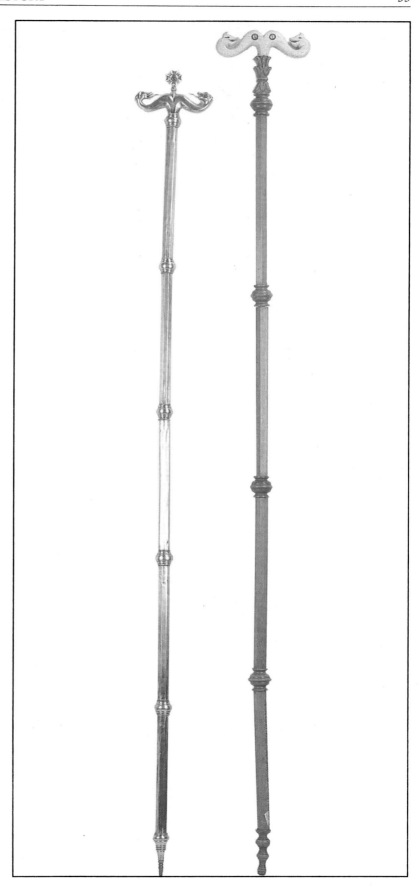

46. Bishop's crosier, 18th-19th century, light profile wood, bone, stones, length 178 cm, invt. No 29065

47. Reliquary of St Cosmas, 1803, donor's inscription, silver, gilding, filigree, reliefs, 23/21.5 cm, invt. No 29188

48. Offertory plate featuring the Virgin Orant, 1818, donor's inscription, silver, diam. 38 cm, invt. No 29209

49 A. Reliquary - offertory box, 1812, outer appearance - silver and dark-red velvet, 34.5/19.5/7 cm, invt. No 29198

49 B. Reliquary - offertory box,
1821, inner appearance - SS Constantine and Hellen, St Paraskeva
and others, cross, silver, gilding,
34.5/19.5/7 cm, invt. No 29198

50. Reliquary of St Matrona with scenes from the life, 1811, donor's inscription, silver, gilding, 21.5/20.5/22 cm, invt. No 29116

51. Repousse of a skull, 1811, silver, gilding, filigree, color stones, enamel, invt. No 29116

52 A. Reliquary - offertory box, 1821, outer appearance - silver, blue velvet and appliques, 32/ 28.5/8 cm, invt. No 29098

52 B. Reliquary - offertory box,
1821, inner side an icon Our Lady
of Tenderness and a cross, silver,
gilding, inscription, 32/28.5/8 cm,
invt. No 29098

53. Gospel with repousse, publ.
Athens, 1832, silver, gilding, with
a box of dark red velvet, 11/7.5/
2.5 cm, invt. No 13666

54. Reliquary featuring archbishop Dionysius of Constantinople, 1820, donor's inscription,
goldsmith Dimiter, silver alloy
with gilding, filigree, corals, color
stones, 20.5/17.5 cm, invt. No
29276

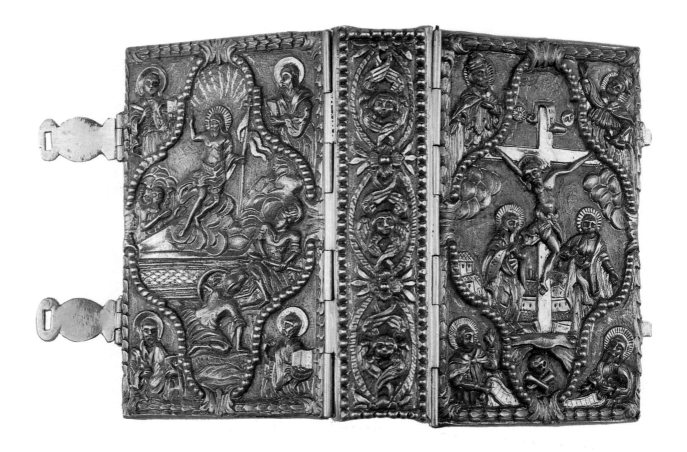

55. Pyx featuring the Holy Seven, 1833, donor's inscription, silver, gilding, ht. 52.5 cm, diam. 27 cm, invt. No 29114

56. Repousse to an icon of the Virgin, 1831, silver alloy, color stones, 25/19 cm, invt. No 29083

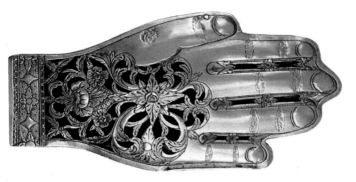

57. Reliquary, the Lamentation, St Nedelya, St Nahum, St Clement, St Nicholas, St Haralampi, 1837, donor's inscription, silver, 27/16.5/15.5 cm, invt. No 29193

58. Inner parts for the relics of a reliquary, 1837, silver, floral ornament, 2 objects, 18/10 cm, 12.5 cm, invt. No 29193

59. Repousse to an icon of the Virgin of Kikska, 1831, donor's inscription, silver alloy with gilding, 16/12 cm, invt. No 29182

60. Gospel with repousse, publ.
Vienna 1857, gilded brass plates
on red velvet binding, 26/38/4 cm,
invt. No 12558

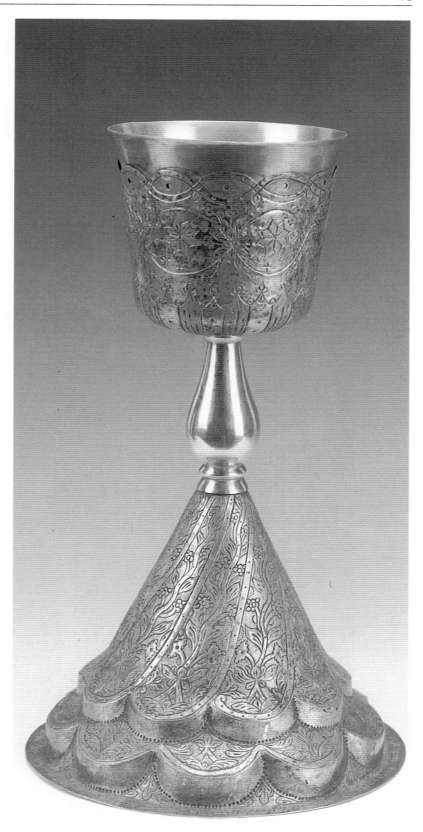

61. Chalice, 1864, silver, gilding,
donor's inscription, ht. 31 cm,
invt. No 33879

62. Gospel with repousse featuring The Crucifixion and The Descent into Hell, publ. Venice, 1864, silver, gilding, 11.3/9/2.5 cm, invt. No 29063

63. Censer, 1870, inscription in Bulgarian, brass, silver coating, ht. 15 cm, diam. 8 cm, invt. No 16873

64. Rhipide, 1876, from the village of Kainardja, Silistra district, silver alloy, relief decoration, diam. 17 cm, invt. No 31377

65. Altar cross, 1883, from Pancharevo, ten scenes from the Feasts of Jesus Christ, wood carving, repousse, silver alloy, 19.5/6 cm, invt. No 224100

66. Cross, 1888, donor's inscription, silver alloy, ht. 31 cm, invt. No 33289

67. Chalice, 1892, donor's inscription, from the Church of St George in the village of Sotochino, floral ornamentation, silver alloy, 24/10 cm, invt. No 33879

68. Votive object featuring an oxen-drawn cart, early 19th century, from the village of Mladinovo, Haskovo district, silver alloy, 12.5/16.5 cm, invt. No 14695

69. Votive statues from the spring at the Arapovski Monastery, Plovdiv district, 19th century, copper alloy with silver coating, 11 objects., invt. No 26105

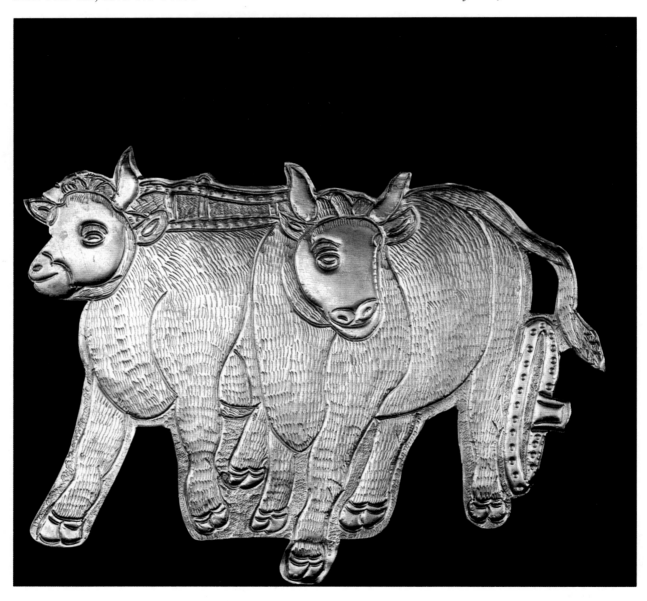

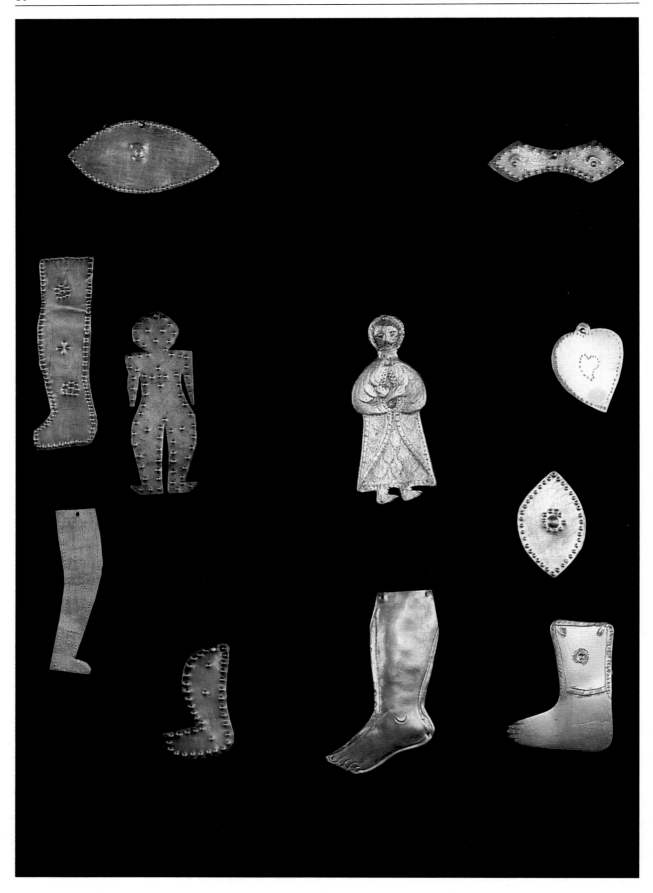

70. Votive objects, 19th century, from different regions of Bulgaria, copper alloy with silver coating, 11 objects, invt. No 12866, 12872, 12871, 31817, 12864, 26105/12, 31812, 31811, 12868, 12870

71. Votive crown from an icon of the Virgin, 19th century, from the Troyan Monastery, silver alloy with gilding, fretwork, 17/11.5 cm, invt. No 33125

73. Altar cross featuring The Crucifixion and The Baptism, 19th
century, wood carving, repousse,
silver alloy, 11/22 cm, invt. No
21031

72. Censer, 19th century, bronze,
27/15 cm, invt. No 29100

74. Lamp, 19th century, silver alloy, filigree, ht. 19 cm, diam. 7 cm, invt. No 29532

75. Cross featuring The Crucifixion and The Baptism, 19th century, wood carving, repousse, silver alloy, 19/8.5 cm, invt. No 29164

76. Gospels with repousse, the four evangelists, 19th century, silver, gilding, 10.5/12 cm, invt. No 29576/ a-b 31326, 4 objects

77. Communion bread print, 19th century, W Bulgaria, initials of Jesus Christ, two-sided, wood, carving, diam. 11.3 cm, invt. No 32184

78. Communion bread print, 19th
century, W Bulgaria, initials of
Jesus Christ, two-sided, wood,
carving, 11.2/12 cm, invt. No
18729

79. Unction box featuring Christ
the Ruler of the Universe, 19th
century, silver alloy, relief decoration, 5.4/4 cm, invt. No 30441

80. Lamp, 19th century, with engraved donor's inscription, silver alloy, ht. 14.5 cm, diam. 9.5 cm, invt. No 29531

81. Lamp, 19th century, silver alloy, ht. 19 cm, diam. 11 cm, invt. No 29149

82. Repousses from the back binding of a gospel, 19th century, silver alloy, 15/12.5 cm, invt. No 29096, 2 objects

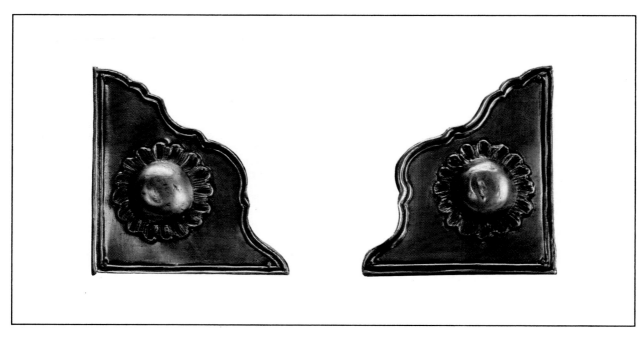

83. Repousses from the front cover of a gospel, 19th century, silver alloy, 9.5/8.5 cm, invt. No 29179

84. Communion bread print, 19th
century, W Bulgaria, initials of
Jesus Christ, two-sided, wood,
carving, 6.5/7.2 cm, invt. No
11029

85. Chalice, 19th century, with
floral and geometric motifs, relief incisions of the Virgin, Jesus
Christ, John the Precursor and the
Crucifixion in four medallions, silver alloy, size 25/14.5 cm, invt.
No 34104

86. Chalice, 19th century, donor's inscription, reliefs, silver, gilding, nielo, ht. 34 cm, invt. No 29066

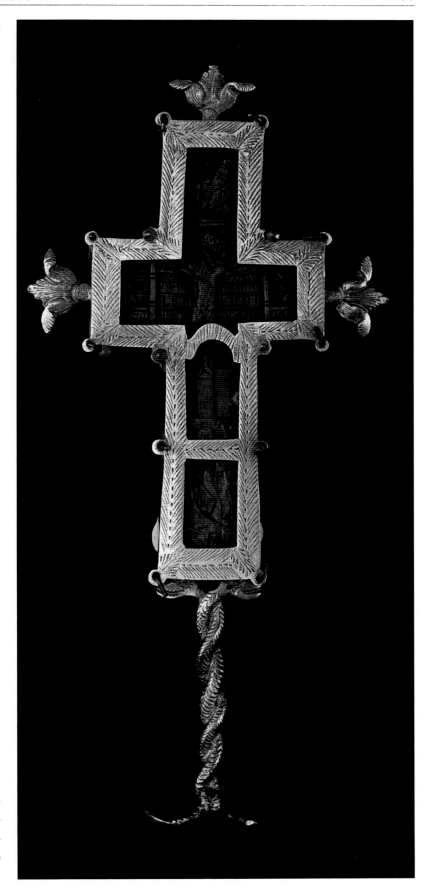

87. Cross featuring The Crucifixion and The Baptism, 19th century, wood carving, repousse, silver alloy, 18/8.5 cm, invt. No 29162

88. Chalice, 19th century, floral and geometric motif, silver alloy, 24/11 cm, invt. No 34106

89. Rhipide featuring the Holy Trinity, mid-19th century, village of Shtit, Haskovo region, silver 27/50 cm, invt. No 7454/a

90. Communion bread print, 19th century, W Bulgaria, initials of Jesus Christ, two-sided, wood, carving, 9.8/8.6 cm, invt. No 32185

91. Chalice, silver alloy, gilding,
ht. 28 cm, invt. No 33303

92. Lamp, 19th century, donor's inscription, cherubim, fretwork, silver alloy, ht. 12 cm, diam. 7 cm, invt. No 29133

93. Gospel with repousse featuring The Crucifixion, the four evangelists, 19th century, 14.5/20 cm, 15.5/11.5, invt. No 20331, 5 objects

94. Lamp, 19th century, silver alloy, ht. 12 cm, diam. 7 cm, invt. No 29148

95. Chalice, 19th century, donor's inscription reliefs, silver, gilding, ht. 27 cm, invt. No 34102

96. Cross, 19th century, miniature
wood carving, silver, gilding, filigree, color stones, 28.5/14 cm,
invt. No 29181

97. Cross, 19th century, featuring
The Crucifixion and The Baptism,
wood carving, silver alloy with
gilding, green glass stones, 27/9
cm, invt. No 29172

98. Bishop's miter, 19th century,
brass, gilding, stones, medallions
with the four evangelists, wood,
tempera, ht. 27 cm, diam. 18 cm,
invt. No 29205

99. Cross, 19th century, silver, filigree, miniature wood carving,
color stones, ht. 40 cm, invt. No
33534

A LIST OF THE ILLUSTRATIONS

1. Rhipide Christ the Ruler of the Universe, 1594, donor's inscription, silver, gilding, enamel, diam. 23 cm, invt. No 29216
2. Rhipides, 16th century, featuring Christ the Great Prelate and Christ Emmanuel, silver alloy, nielo, enamel, 43/31 cm, invt. No 29207
3. Rhipides, 16th century, featuring Christ the Great Prelate and Christ Emmanuel, silver alloy, nielo, enamel, 43/31 cm, invt. No 29207
4. Rhipide Christ Emmanuel, 1594, donor's inscription, silver, gilding, enamel, diam. 23 cm, invt. No 29216
5. Cross, 1615, donor's inscription, master hieromonk Averki, miniature wood carving, silver with gilding, inlaid stones, 8.5/21/3 cm, invt. No 29153
6. Cross, 1618, donor's inscription, wood carving, repousse of silver alloy with gilding, 35/12.5 cm, invt. No 29173
7. Pyx, 1626, Dechani Monastery, silver, gilding, enamel, color stones, Chiprovtsi goldsmithery school, size 30/25 cm, invt. No 29211
8. Reliquary, 1630, featuring The Ascension, silver alloy with gilding, 26.5/19/6.5 cm, invt. No 29174
9. Cross, 1648, donor's inscription, master Kaspar, commissioned by the town of Seres, miniature wood carving, repousse of gold-plated filigree, coral, 13/29/2.5 cm, invt. No 29175
10. Cross, 17th century, miniature wood carving, repousse with gold-plated filigree, color stone, cellular enamel, in a wooden box, 29.5/16.5 cm, invt. No 29186
11. Repousse of an icon of St George with scenes from his life, 17th century, silver alloy with gilding, diam. 25 cm, invt. No 29047
12. Reliquary of St Dionysius the Patriarch of Constantinople with scenes from the Bible and saints, 1744, donor's inscription, silver, gilding, 31/23/27 cm, invt. No 29115
13. Repousse of a skull, death mask, 1744, silver, gilding, nielo, invt. No 29115
14. Chalice, 1731, donor's inscription, silver, gilding, floral motifs and birds, ht. 26 cm, invt. No 29067
15. Censer, 1763, donor's inscription, silver, ht. 23.5 cm, diam. 11.5 cm, invt. No 29136
16. Reliquary featuring Christ the Ruler of the Universe and SS Constantine and Hellen, 1765, silver alloy with gilding, relief decoration, 30.5/14/3.5 cm, invt. No 29168
17. Repousse of the icon The Virgin Showing the Way, 1765, silver alloy, 108/60 cm, invt. No 29041
18. Reliquary whose lid features the Holy Trinity, 1773, silver alloy, plastic decoration, 34/29/7 cm, invt. No 29210
19. Cross, 1774, donor's inscription, master Konstantin Stoyanov, miniature carving, repousse, gold-plated filigree, color stones, 28.5/12.5 cm, invt. No 29178
20. Lamp, 1776, silver, ht. 68 cm, invt. No 29213
21. Reliquary, St Dionysius, St John Chrysostom, St Pantaleimon, St Andrew the First Called, 1783, donor's inscription, silver, gilding, copper base, 25.5/18/10 cm, invt. No 29194
22. Cross, 1786, silver, gilding, color stones and corals, 57/23 cm, invt. No 29185
23. Service vessel featuring The Baptism of Christ and The Virgin with Apostles, 1787, donor's inscription, master Nikolaya, silver, gilding, ht. 32 cm, diam. 27.5 cm, invt. No 29124, 29126
24. Lamp, 1789, donor's inscription. silver, ht. 40 cm, diam. 24 cm, invt. No 29212
25. Repousse to an icon of the Virgin, 1789, silver alloy, color stones, 28/20 cm, invt. No 29082
26. Repousse of the icon of John the Precursor, 18th century, silver alloy, 84/64 cm, invt. No 29042
27. Cross, 18th century, wood carving, repousse from silver alloy, corals, 16/9 cm, invt. No 29161
28. Reliquary of St Haralampi, 18th century, donor's inscription, silver, gilding, 9/6/2 cm, invt. No 29167
29. Repousse to an icon of the Virgin, 18th century, silver alloy with gilding, color stones, 22.5/17 cm, invt. No 29184
30. Repousse to an icon of Our Lady of Tenderness, 18th century, silver alloy with gilding, color stones, 27.5/20.5 cm, invt. No 29183
31. Cross, 18th century donor's inscription, silver, gilding, stones, 67/30 cm, invt. No 29189
32. Reliquary, 18th century, silver, gilding, 11.5/4.5/3.5 cm, invt. No 29166
33. Cross, 18th century, silver, gilding, Christ's feasts, 22/13.5 cm, invt. No 29131
34. Repousse featuring St John the Precursor with scenes from his life, 18th century, silver, gilding. 150/130 cm, invt. No 29054, 29053
35. Reliquary, 18th century, silver, gilding, donor's inscription, 16/6.5/2.5 cm, invt. No 29163
36. Reliquary of St Dionysius, 18th century, donor's inscription, silver, gilding, 18.5/5.5/3.5 cm, invt. No 29156
37. Bishop's crosier, 18th century, black lacquered wood, silver, gilding, length 165 cm, invt. No 29197
38. Reliquary of St Trifon, 18th century, donor's inscription, silver, gilding, 18.5/5.5/4 cm, invt. No 29155
39. Bishop's belt featuring The Virgin with Prophets, second half of the 18th century, 13 plates, silver, gilding, length 74 cm, invt. No 29075
40. Lamp, second half of the 18th century, silver alloy, 19/10.5 cm, invt. No 29146
41. Lamp, second half of the 18th century, silver, ht. 22 cm, diam. 10.5 cm, invt. No 29140
42. Censer, 18th-19th century, silver, copper, ht. 25 cm, diam. 12 cm, invt. No 29130
43. Cross, 18th-19th century, gilded filigree, granulation, stones, 8/16 cm, invt. No 29962
44. Reliquary - offertory box, with an icon the Virgin Showing the Way, 18th-19th century, wood, tempera, repousse, silver, gilding, 13/10.5/2.5 cm, invt. No 29191
45. Bishop's crosier, 18th-19th century, light profile wood, bone, stones, length 178 cm, invt. No 29065
46. Bishop's crosier, 19th century, brass, gilding, stones, length 170 cm, invt. No 29105
47. Reliquary of St Cosmas, 1803, donor's inscription, silver, gilding, filigree, reliefs, 23/21.5 cm, invt. No 29188
48. Offertory plate featuring the Virgin Orant, 1818, donor's inscription, silver, diam. 38 cm, invt. No 29209
49 A. Reliquary - offertory box, 1812, outer appearance - silver and dark-red velvet, 34.5/19.5/7 cm, invt. No 29198
49 B. Reliquary - offertory box, 1821, inner appearance - SS Constantine and Hellen, St Paraskeva and others, cross, silver, gilding, 34.5/19.5/7 cm, invt. No 29198
50. Reliquary of St Matrona with scenes from the life, 1811, donor's inscription, silver, gilding, 21.5/20.5/22 cm, invt. No 29116
51. Repousse of a skull, 1811, silver, gilding, filigree, color stones, enamel, invt. No 29116

52 A. Reliquary - offertory box, 1821, outer appearance - silver, blue velvet and appliques, 32/28.5/8 cm, invt. No 29098

52 B. Reliquary - offertory box, 1821, inner side an icon Our Lady of Tenderness and a cross, silver, gilding, inscription, 32/28.5/8 cm, invt. No 29098

53. Gospel with repousse, publ. Athens, 1832, silver, gilding, with a box of dark red velvet, 11/7.5/2.5 cm, invt. No 13666

54. Reliquary featuring archbishop Dionysius of Constantinople, 1820, donor's inscription, goldsmith Dimiter, silver alloy with gilding, filigree, corals, color stones, 20.5/17.5 cm, invt. No 29276

55. Pyx featuring the Holy Seven, 1833, donor's inscription, silver, gilding, ht. 52.5 cm, diam. 27 cm, invt. No 29114

56. Repousse to an icon of the Virgin, 1831, silver alloy, color stones, 25/19 cm, invt. No 29083

57. Reliquary, the Lamentation, St Nedelya, St Nahum, St Clement, St Nicholas, St Haralampi, 1837, donor's inscription, silver, 27/16.5/15.5 cm, invt. No 29193

58. Inner parts for the relics of a reliquary, 1837, silver, floral ornament, 2 objects, 18/10 cm, 12.5 cm, invt. No 29193

59. Repousse to an icon of the Virgin of Kikska, 1831, donor's inscription, silver alloy with gilding, 16/12 cm, invt. No 29182

60. Gospel with repousse, publ. Vienna 1857, gilded brass plates on red velvet binding, 26/38/4 cm, invt. No 12558

61. Chalice, 1864, silver, gilding, donor's inscription, ht. 31 cm, invt. No 33879

62. Gospel with repousse featuring The Crucifixion and The Descent into Hell, publ. Venice, 1864, silver, gilding, 11.3/9/2.5 cm, invt. No 29063

63. Censer, 1870, inscription in Bulgarian, brass, silver coating, ht. 15 cm, diam. 8 cm, invt. No 16873

64. Rhipide, 1876, from the village of Kainardja, Silistra district, silver alloy, relief decoration, diam. 17 cm, invt. No 31377

65. Altar cross, 1883, from Pancharevo, ten scenes from the Feasts of Jesus Christ, wood carving, repousse, silver alloy, 19.5/6 cm, invt. No 224100

66. Cross, 1888, donor's inscription, silver alloy, ht. 31 cm, invt. No 33289

67. Chalice, 1892, donor's inscription, from the Church of St George in the village of Sotochino, floral ornamentation, silver alloy, 24/10 cm, invt. No 33879

68. Votive object featuring an oxen-drawn cart, early 19th century, from the village of Mladinovo, Haskovo district, silver alloy, 12.5/16.5 cm, invt. No 14695

69. Votive statues from the spring at the Arapovski Monastery, Plovdiv district, 19th century, copper alloy with silver coating, 11 objects., invt. No 26105

70. Votive objects, 19th century, from different regions of Bulgaria, copper alloy with silver coating, 11 objects, invt. No 12866, 12872, 12871, 31817, 12864, 26105/12, 31812, 31811, 12868, 12870

71. Votive crown from an icon of the Virgin, 19th century, from the Troyan Monastery, silver alloy with gilding, fretwork, 17/11.5 cm, invt. No 33125

72. Censer, 19th century, bronze, 27/15 cm, invt. No 29100

73. Altar cross featuring The Crucifixion and The Baptism, 19th century, wood carving, repousse, silver alloy, 11/22 cm, invt. No 21031

74. Lamp, 19th century, silver alloy, filigree, ht. 19 cm, diam. 7 cm, invt. No 29532

75. Cross featuring The Crucifixion and The Baptism, 19th century, wood carving, repousse, silver alloy, 19/8.5 cm, invt. No 29164

76. Gospels with repousse, the four evangelists, 19th century, silver, gilding, 10.5/12 cm, invt. No 29576/ a-b 31326, 4 objects

77. Communion bread print, 19th century, W Bulgaria, initials of Jesus Christ, two-sided, wood, carving, diam. 11.3 cm, invt. No 32184

78. Communion bread print, 19th century, W Bulgaria, initials of Jesus Christ, two-sided, wood, carving, 11.2/12 cm, invt. No 18729

79. Unction box featuring Christ the Ruler of the Universe, 19th century, silver alloy, relief decoration, 5.4/4 cm, invt. No 30441

80. Lamp, 19th century, with engraved donor's inscription, silver alloy, ht. 14.5 cm, diam. 9.5 cm, invt. No 29531

81. Lamp, 19th century, silver alloy, ht. 19 cm, diam. 11 cm, invt. No 29149

82. Repousses from the back binding of a gospel, 19th century, silver alloy, 15/12.5 cm, invt. No 29096, 2 objects

83. Repousses from the front cover of a gospel, 19th century, silver alloy, 9.5/8.5 cm, invt. No 29179

84. Communion bread print, 19th century, W Bulgaria, initials of Jesus Christ, two-sided, wood, carving, 6.5/7.2 cm, invt. No 11029

85. Chalice, 19th century, with floral and geometric motifs, relief incisions of the Virgin, Jesus Christ, John the Precursor and the Crucifixion in four medallions, silver alloy, size 25/14.5 cm, invt. No 34104

86. Chalice, 19th century, donor's inscription, reliefs, silver, gilding, nielo, ht. 34 cm, invt. No 29066

87. Cross featuring The Crucifixion and The Baptism, 19th century, wood carving, repousse, silver alloy, 18/8.5 cm, invt. No 29162

88. Chalice, 19th century, floral and geometric motif, silver alloy, 24/11 cm, invt. No 34106

89. Rhipide featuring the Holy Trinity, mid-19th century, village of Shtit, Haskovo region, silver 27/50 cm, invt. No 7454/a

90. Communion bread print, 19th century, W Bulgaria, initials of Jesus Christ, two-sided, wood, carving, 9.8/8.6 cm, invt. No 32185

91. Chalice, silver alloy, gilding, ht. 28 cm, invt. No 33303

92. Lamp, 19th century, donor's inscription, cherubim, fretwork, silver alloy, ht. 12 cm, diam. 7 cm, invt. No 29133

93. Gospel with repousse featuring The Crucifixion, the four evangelists, 19th century, 14.5/20 cm, 15.5/11.5, invt. No 20331, 5 objects

94. Lamp, 19th century, silver alloy, ht. 12 cm, diam. 7 cm, invt. No 29148

95. Chalice, 19th century, donor's inscription reliefs, silver, gilding, ht. 27 cm, invt. No 34102

96. Cross, 19th century, miniature wood carving, silver, gilding, filigree, color stones, 28.5/14 cm, invt. No 29181

97. Cross, 19th century, featuring The Crucifixion and The Baptism, wood carving, silver alloy with gilding, green glass stones, 27/9 cm, invt. No 29172

98. Bishop's miter, 19th century, brass, gilding, stones, medallions with the four evangelists, wood, tempera, ht. 27 cm, diam. 18 cm, invt. No 29205

99. Cross, 19th century, silver, filigree, miniature wood carving, color stones, ht. 40 cm, invt. No 33534

Front cover: Baptism – central scene on one side
of the woodcarving of the gonfalon cross, 19th century

Back cover: Reliquary of St Cosmas, 1803

Teofana Matakieva-Lilkova

CHURCH PLATE
FROM THE COLLECTIONS
OF THE NATIONAL MUSEUM OF HISTORY

Photographer: Dimiter Angelov
Artist: Antoniy Handjiysky
Editor: Vyara Kandjeva
English Translation: Roumiana Delcheva

BORINA Publishing House
P.O.Box 105; 1408 Sofia, Bulgaria

ISBN 954 500 061 9

Printed by K & M Publishing Co